To HELL And BACK

A Life in Addiction and Recovery in Poem

Steven L. Massé

 FriesenPress

One Printers Way
Altona, MB R0G 0B0
Canada

www.friesenpress.com

Copyright © 2022 by Steven L. Massé
First Edition — 2022

Edited by Paul C.

ISBN
978-1-03-914447-7 (Hardcover)
978-1-03-914446-0 (Paperback)
978-1-03-914448-4 (eBook)

1. POETRY

Distributed to the trade by The Ingram Book Company

TABLE OF CONTENTS

CONTROLLING MASTER

We all have a master, mine is cruel.
I call mine my "Friend", my fuel.
It comes in all sizes and shapes.
In using it, there are no escapes.

My "Friend" is a really controlling one.
It's my lifelong disease that I can't outrun.
It is there for fun and then to make me hurt.
It wants everything from me, until I'm in the dirt.

At first it was fun to laugh and play.
Always in pain, I couldn't keep it at bay.
It is smarter than I, in every way.
I couldn't hide, it found me everyday.

When I tell it to leave, be gone.
It knows that I am one of its pawns.
I will lie, deceive, and steal to find it.
It had me to the core, I had to admit.

It wants to take all and spend eternity with me.
Sends me out alone, on a raft drifting in the sea.
It was there for instant gratification, and not to feel.
I tried to run but it told me "that's not in our deal"

While my "Friend" lives on with me, I barely exist.
Loves loss, financial ruin and still continues to persist.
Wants more, it's my controlling master, that no one takes seriously.
It will always have and own me and help live a life so dangerously.

GOODBYE

My thoughts and fears now spoken
It is now time to be honesty open
My "Upstairs" is totally crowded
My dreams of tomorrow clouded

Have endured hell in lost and pain
Anything you say would be in vain
You listened and tried, it is not your fault
I have these demons locked in my vault

My two beautiful girl's need a dad
I'm no better than what they had
I'm angry, I'm sad, and I'm lost
I need to escape my holocaust

So sorry to all as this is short
This is my plan, not to abort
Myove to all and God bless
I'm leaving before I leave a mess

PAIN

It's not a made up word
When hurt rises to the unheard
Aches and tears abound
A place of joy drowned

Feeling your palm being clawed
Toes curled, tears flow, no facade
Endured daily, leads to an internal demon
Fighting daily, peace taken from this free man

Mental being in a sky of darkness
Feels like knife stabbing, no stillness
Many forms of pain, has no boundaries
It rises above all, now scarred memories

It will forever exist, no escape
Born with it, ages and takes shape
Endured unpleasantly by us and all creatures
Left alone, not one of our enjoyable features

It is not to be ignored, but embraced
Solved, it is a problem affliction erased
Your stronger, continue to be alive
Put your best foot forward and strive

SHAME

This word haunts me. A broken soul
Mistakes made. I couldn't control
Hard to think, as memories abound
A deep hate felt by all around

Will my deep pain last forever
No more that I can say however
The immense pain caused to those
It is something, I wouldn't have chose

Guilt and shame, excruciating feelings of failure
Mistakes in my journey, unfortunate behavior
Amends, peace, tranquility, all in good time
Work to be done, it's all part of the climb

Never to be forgotten by others
They are my errors, not others
That is yesterday, I think not
I can't, as that battle I fought

UNDERSTANDING

What makes a person an alcoholic and addict.
Reality of most people, we are just a derelict
Appears that no one really cares or knows
Men and women suffering a life they never chose

Live a minute in one of these unfortunate souls
Born a success, raised possibly without any goals
A paper bag over a bottle recently bought
Creating yesterday without a second thought

It's not what it appears, so open your eyes and ears
We go through life in a blur, fighting all our fears
I am one of the millions that suffer from this affliction
Addiction is permanent, unfortunately this is not fiction

When you see an addict, YOU see a bum, a loser, and a lowlife
Possibly one time that person worked, had kids and even a wife
You don't know his upbringing, his education, even his name
Yet you judge him, while they are busy living a life of shame

Awake your mind, you are definitely no different than us
If I would say that in public, it would raise such a fuss
It's true the world round but few people ever admit it
Many addictions but we are the ones who appear a misfit

We are human, we love, cry, and get angry
We often go adrift, intoxicated, lonely and hungry
But you need to know none of it is planned
So it is all your turn, to try and understand

Now is time to start a change of thinking
Get your heart and mind to start a reprinting
Look deep into our eyes, see our hurt and pain
What's there for you to lose, but only to gain

OPENING COMMENTS

As I am now, being sober and an onion being peeled!

These poems reflect 46 years of my struggle and how I dealt with it. It also describes the health issues, lost loves, family and financial issues but also describes my fight. To be positive every minute, yesterday is dead!

I was lying in a hospital bed as usual and POW!! It hit me. Write! I never wrote before, but the walls started to crumble. The truth was on paper. I felt a new purpose, exposed but words to help! This is my life. Don't choose it! Learn from my words, as I learn more about me with every stroke of a pen.

In the poems, I will make reference to " Friend" or "Friends". They refer to your DOC (Drug Of Choice). Mine just happened to be forty-six years of hell drinking, so alcohol was my "Friend". At times I had multiple "Friends". Beer, hard (hard liquor), hash, hash oil, weed, edibles, Percs, Hydro, and Thirty-three prescription pills taken daily. Including painkillers, muscle relaxants, and sleeping pills. As well the word "Upstairs" will be included. It refers to your head/brain.

Please take your time and feel my energy in every word and get a mental image. The poems are in this order as that was how I was feeling that minute. The feelings started to flow as I wrote. I hope it moves you, helps you or someone in your circle, as there are a staggering millions of us suffering from mental illness, homelessness and addiction.

LIVING IN HELL

How many times did I stare to heaven?
I wanted death, I turned twenty-seven
My "Friend" I love you, why? Don't know
Saw you everyday, putting me in a glow

Was twelve when we met that night
I tasted your nectar, then I took flight
Time and time again, I needed more
The bottle at my lips, no need to pour

"Wrote you letters, called your name
You kept me here, a life of shame
God I prayed, you never heard well
"Hear me! Take me, I'm Living in Hell!"

Wanted my feelings to disappear
I reached out and found you here
The hurt vanished, but soon returned
I couldn't hide them, I quickly learned

Was just one of your pawns played
I tried to run, but my Friend I stayed
As a child, saw a glimpse of who I am
Became a lost soul living on the lam

"Wrote you letters, called your name
You kept me here, a life of shame
God I prayed, you never heard well
"Hear me! Take me! I'm Living in Hell!"

I focused on you, the only friend I had
Living constantly numb, I had gone mad
My liar's chair long worn itself useless
A minister of death, you became ruthless

You left me alone but had my devotion
Often pondered death, what an emotion
Forty-six long years later, I was still a drunk
Time for a change, wasn't yet tossed as junk

"Wrote you letters, called your name
You kept me here, a life of shame
God I prayed, you never heard well
"Hear me! Take me! I'm Living in Hell!"

I had no strength left, I needed out
You had me then, without any doubt
That was then, I'm now sober day by day
Good bye Friend, until the end I will pray

THE TEENS

Was born and raised in Quebec,
on the beautiful St. Lawrence River.
I love the smell of the saltwater, AHH! Seafood and beaches!
My "Friend", I had not met! Parents home socials, cleanup, I deliver.
Drink Samples taken. Whoosh! Pleasure! Laughing, feeling Regis.

I was twelve years old, when my "Friend" and I first united.
Parents' socials still. I tried leftover drinks, some of dad's stuff.
A hook well set! I was captured! Was no longer clear-sighted.
My unknown future, I never imagined it would be so rough.

I was able to find my "Friend" on my own, as money talks!
Weekends, always impaired, staggering walk, never enough!
The parties, dances, bonfires, alone and terrifying long walks.
Morning came, Christ! Head always hurt and I was feeling rough.

My grades were good, great buddies, girls, sports and my family.
My drinking escalated, money was needed, I got a job, got a pay.
"Friend" alcohol met "Friend" Hash, instant love, the two a calamity.
Run from it? Why not? I was chained, was busy creating yesterday.

Summer home, beach fires, guitar tunes, all good times.
There were two bars, open 'til? Sunup as I walked home.
How did I get away with this? Committing journey crimes.
Girls met, my "Friend" helped, no nerves, it's all in the tone.

Summer job, I biked 6 km. I was still high and drunk.
In the barn I loaded hay. I felt like shit but, sweating it out.
Day after day! One was never one! Started to feel sunk.
In trouble! My drinking had taken an insane amount of sprout!

The one that got away, beauty! She visited my neighbor.
Unfortunately, my "Friend" was powerless over her spell.
Could not act on my feelings, needed that moment to savor!
I failed, she got away! Now these feelings are added to my hell.

I was always the drunkest, "piss-tank", I easily earned that title.
Graduate year, I picked up the pace, my tolerance was rising!
My two "Friends", they were best buds, the two were always vital.
College, the learning chapter, my "Friends" and I did
the organizing!

THE LEARNING CHAPTER

I was free! A little scared! Sault College for three years.
Residence, in room 101.It was huge! No roommate.
Had classes, homework and sports. It was time for a few beers!
Shit! My "Friend" and I reunited! Bedtime was always late.

Went to learn. That's what I did.
Good student, but always in a haze.
Met buddies, pub night, parties, my room, we did gather.
"Friend" hash disappeared; oil took its place. The next phase.
Twenty-four, oil galore. I needed help! I was tired, every night
a cadaver.

Not Enough! I needed more! Introducing the Purple Lantern.
Watering hole it was, ten minutes there, twenty back.
Thirty cent draft, I filled myself. Now starting a deadly pattern.
Got to my room for more "Friends", then I went black.

Watering hole two, the same walks, unfortunately the same result.
Fifty-five cents, fifty-five brand, for fifty-five minutes, I was all in!
Walked home. Morning arose, I felt grass!
Someone's lawn, my fault.
Study? No! My "Friends" always gathered,
fucked-up just a smidgen!

Never enough! Hard liquor it was. Twenty-six to start, then to forty.
Felt elevated, added euphoria with "Friends",
partying away my youth.
Twenty-four and my watering holes, hard and oil,
I was no longer dorky.
At night's end, I was always making love to my Rye and Vermouth.

Final year I grabbed a home. Pardee Avenue it was.
The Party always lived at Pardee, day and night.
Hash reunited. Hot knives. I was High! It was unanimous!
Buddies around, with all my "Friends", I took flight!

I had not seen or felt the sunshine for a very long time!
A blur, a reputation formed. PLEASE! I Needed to Stop!!
I gathered "Friends", they came "Upstairs", told of their crime.
Had no plan. A failure to plan is a plan for failure, it was a flop!!

I graduated with good grades, good buddies too!
I was sad, scared, anxious, and happy as well!
My journey continued. How could this be true?
The next chapter, "Friend" free? Or kept living in hell?

DREAM JOB

I landed a permanent job, game warden that is.
The dream life that I studied for. I did not refuse.
I was nervous, had goosebumps on my epidermis.
Summer, in uniform dress, cheeks with red hues

I patrolled the forest on a beautiful sunny day.
I was alone, driving a tree-lined bush road.
It was calming! I was in my element, I must say.
As I drove slowly, where a peaceful river flowed.

Nature is stunning. God's playground in every way!
An oath was taken to protect God's varied creatures.
Rivers, trees, and wildlife are admired every single day.
How could some people ruin all these amazing features?

Day after day, the dream job. Not for the faint of heart!
Very long hours! Exhausted working well into the night.
Morning came. Maybe slept a wink. A new day start.
Fucking poachers were to be caught! I had no fright!

The first two years, I was a mess! Was feeling very hollow.
My "Friend", I was dying inside. Please! I couldn't do this anymore!
I could not lose this dream, as my reputation was sure to follow.
I briefly quit. My demons surfaced and soon my "Friends" were at
my door.

You were let in again and again, but you never listened!
Started the gym, my "Friend" and I were very moderate.
Years later, hard pokes its head in again. It just glistened!
I tried! Powerless! Tried only beer, but hard was predominate.

Firearms, knives, axes as well. All to visually take care.
It was not a job; it was a living! Those working it are thrilled!
Wish daily that I could still be there. It's not fair!
My "Friend" gave me a desk job, so unfortunately, I left unfulfilled.

THE TRAIL

Took a trail one day as it was used.
It was my job to see what was happening.
Someone ahead could be an accused.
The trail was long. There was no slackening.

Day turned into night, I had to stay.
Settled under the trees to wait it out.
Thoughts collected at what I may say.
My training set in. I knew I had the clout.

My flashlight is ready and my thoughts are prepared.
Suddenly, a gunshot was heard in the distance.
My heart pumping, sweat steaming into the air.
Another shot very close. I had no assistance!

Footsteps were close. Voices heard over the knowle.
Moments later, my flashlight shone, command: "STOP"
My heart was pounding! Only to see a very large hole,
It was the loaded firearm barrel, pointed at my TOP!

My sidearm drawn, they were commanded to drop.
There were three men, and I was only ONE!
The only firearm went down immediately. PLOP!
My loud vocal orders worked! That time I WON!!

TRAUMA

Never working in white, always yellow, orange,
or red which is on the brink.
White is dangerous. To be Alert, eyes open, feeling it in your core.
Never had tombstone courage. Safety number one,
I always had to think.
Long hours, extensive training, and drunks, this job was no chore.

Patrolling one summer day. Dust flying ahead, OH NO! Rollover!
Van in shrubs. Oh shit! It's empty! Jump? It didn't drive itself.
Parts found, he was face down, in the shrubbery. He was all over!
His main body was found meters from his head, I lost myself!

On my way home, in front of a car, WTF! It swerves!
Car versus transport, many pieces! It stopped inches from me.
Moans were heard. She was deceased. Ohhhh! My nerves!
Young child removed. I held him, comforted while he cried a plea!

Spring it is. Fiddleheads, creepers, and high water. Life emerges.
My favorite sunny spring day. The smell, peaceful. Whoa! A car.
It was parked. Took a trail. Shit! A hanging corpse. Puking urges!
Assistance called. My statement given. It was the worst day by far.

These trauma's above and others are buried in my core.
I needed relief.
My "Friend" never failed to help! Always a forty and a twenty-six.
Drank that everyday. My traumas were deep. I was in full disbelief.
More hooks added to my core. I was prepared as I had my daily fix.

RAMPING UP CHAPTER

Became an investigator. In plain clothes and had a vehicle too!
Training, teaching, planning investigations,
delving deep into your life.
Time away, Ah! Who am I kidding, everyday!
Drank heavily and off I flew. My "Friend" leave!
I've got a job to do, you're taking me to the afterlife.

Love lost!, lies galore, fuck!
How could my lies get me out of this one?
To Toronto, rehab, for three weeks, I have to! My work agrees.
I graduated, I was sober, got my wife back, ! My worst was to come!
It took me back, harder than ever!
Two sixties, my "Friend" had all my keys.

The day I dreaded the most hit me hard but I knew it was coming.
Was put off work as I was sick.
Toronto rehab reunited, finished and left.
Closest liquor, on-route home.
Woke up in car, showing all my plumbing.
How was I still alive! WTF my "Friend".
Feeling like I had committed theft.

Truly alone and at home, I commenced going in my "Upstairs".
A dark and gloomy place, where pain and suffering lay dormant.
Some came to surface. I panicked, so I ordered my "Friend" in pairs.
Covid came, it changed the world but I still have my impairment.

Just before Covid, the hospital visits really commenced!
My body was starting to fail and I didn't have a spare.
Oh! The cycle of self destruction! I was now feeling fenced!
Medications, my "Friend" and I left me in utter despair!

I couldn't stop as my "Friend" and I were inseparable.
News that I had no functioning liver and my kidneys were dead.
Still my spinning rolodex of "Friends" were indispensable.
Barely surviving. I needed to get off that ride but couldn't be lead.

INSANITY

One hospital stay after another, 200 days out of 365, slow learner!
Five day detox, I'm shaking, sweating, Fuck I wanted a drink!
Doctors and nurses, warnings received,
but they know I'm a returner.
All resources set up, discharged, cab to liquor store, I didn't think

My "Friend" you had me. How can I manage to save my dignity?
I pretended to be great to all. They knew! The urge was powerful!
Daily alcohol intake at near death levels,
but I loved it unconditionally
I thought one day the demons would weaken but then,
it was doubtful.

I kept to the cycle. Only path I knew,
even when told I was gonna die.
I isolated, shared all my demons deep within my core
with my "Friends".
A look around, pig pen! Not showered, oftentimes,
I breakdown and cry.
I gave up, I was nobody, just slowly watching
my life pass through a lens.

Kids started finding my "Friend" Vodka,
throwing my love to the curb.
I would run out! Panic set in, the shakes started, I needed a fix.
I would wait for ten and be at the door, stocked up!
Now not to disturb!
There were bottles hidden so well I couldn't find.
Knew of at least six.

My "Friend" you had me imprisoned three times.
Are you done? I continued living the spectrum of human existence.
Pain deeply embedded, I often called dial a bottle lines.
The anguish and loss. Neither mattered
as I watched from a distance.

Why did I continue to do this? Addiction fucking sucks!
The doctors and nurses said I was killing myself,
maybe I had a year!
I was selfish and weak. I had no fight! Using it as a crux.
No happy thoughts. "Upstairs", the cycle deepened,
was on the next tier.

COVID

It came like a mighty freight train,
was on sick leave, stayed at home.
Shutdowns everywhere, finding supplies difficult.
Liquor and beer were essential,
I still had a license and was free to roam.
My children fled. Addictions had affected this adult.

With no kids, it was time for the devil's paintbrush
to start a masterpiece.
Every week, ambulance, detox for days in hospital,
discharge, the cycle!
My "Friend" was patiently waiting, two sixties,
never to ever decrease. They are finished!
I'm shaking, waiting for the opening hour. I was not idle.

My forty-sixth year of abuse, hospitals galore, my organs failing.
I sold the house, moved to an apartment, perfect! Dial a bottle.
Lost my driver's license for medical reasons with my body ailing.
My fingers clasped around my "Friend", then I started to wobble.

Enter new "Friends" hydromorphone,
Ativan, Dopamine and Zopiclone.
Opioids for pain, benzos to tranquilize,
dopamine to elevate, zop to sleep.
The music was always full blast, all "Friends united,
I went to the unknown!
Absolutely nothing and no one to stop me.
I was surely the black-sheep!

I looked at my "Friend" and said,
"I'm tired of being tired, time to go".
From the rim of the bottle, it said, "hahaha! You, I do control"!
I'm Fucked! I guess I let go and continued being the show.
Add my "Friends" cousin, white wine,
now six of them own my soul!

I isolated myself with my "Friends",
everyday turned to night, then to day.
The hamster wouldn't stop spinning its wheel!
I'm in there somewhere.
Police came, wellness check, my "Friends" had played.
so I couldn't say.
I awoke strapped to the emergency bed. An answer to my prayer.

Days seeing doctors and nurses.
It was obvious my "Friends" had to go!
Covid, no visitors, major detox! Daughters called, I was ashamed.
"Daddy" was heard, my heart sank,
"we found a place for you to grow".
Discharged, and daughters said "want dad back",
education to be gained.

FAMILY LIFE

Year thirty-eight of my journey, I met a girl! Delicate like a down
feather. We played ball, I picked her up, and dropped her off,
she wouldn't take NO.
I finally gave in. We got married, had kids
and started living together.
There were new challenges, new loves
but will my "Friend" take it slow?

I stuck then with beer but occasionally I had a hard.
Things were good! Years passed, have two beautiful daughters.
My hard "Friend" started always visiting, without any regard.
Arguments, fighting, late into the night, opening their floodwaters.

Switched from Rye to Vodka in a futile attempt to hide the smell.
Often in the basement, or in shed, thinking I was smart.
Fuck they know!
My girls got older, I am no better.
With my "Friends", It never ended well!
Went to first rehab to save my marriage,
all good, still had demons though!

Six months clean, I struggled, my "Friend" wanted me back,
I gave in.
Went on a long bender!
Got arrested twice for domestic, nothing physical.
Solitary confinement, five days for bail,
my worst nightmare, in a tailspin.
The condition of release, to live in Ottawa,
missing kids, time to be logical!

I went back to rehab but didn't do it for me.
That was a huge mistake.
I got home, my wife left and one of my daughters stayed with dad.
My "Friend" returned, daughter saw my worst,
there was a lot at stake.
She stuck it out for many a year. How and why? She was ironclad!

Then my wife and daughters were gone. What? Both kids and wife?
I was truly alone, I went fucking hard!
Years passed, my body was tired!
Look at what I had! No family, no kids, off sick, a fucking lowlife!
Hospital, my second home, children didn't visit, I wanted to expire.

One rare visit in hospital, one daughter said "Dad you are loved".
As well said "Dad, will you go away and get better"?
How could I say no?
They secured my rehab, bags packed,
I honestly didn't need to be tugged.
It absolutely had been a life changer,
so it was time for my journey to grow!

HOSPITALS

Where do I start? Shit! I have been so many times.
My previous poems were about how my "Friend" affected my life.
My body, and mind were failing! Caught for life crimes.
There is one place, hospital, well taken care of, who needs a wife?

My Kidneys failed, dead they said.
Fuck! Emergency abdominal drain
I became lighter by 8 liters. It was a long stay,
so mom came up to help.
After seventeen days in bed there were signs of life!
Taken with a grain.
All levels were good, I went home, three days later
I'm back with a yelp.

They are my second home, known by the name, The Walking Dead.
My alcohol levels were twice the danger zone.
I was on life twenty two.
Hahaha! I beat the cat! Large hospital,
I am always waiting for a bed.
Like an episode of Cheers.
Everyone knows my name, I'm nothing new.

I sounded drunk and walked the same, legs beet red,
I thought I was fine.
There were people with no legs,
my house full of them, I took pictures.
No one could see them, just me. I fell to the ground
and it wasn't the wine.
Days later I awoke, remembering my name!
I became part of the fixtures.

Liver is dead, toxic poison runs through my veins
and hits my brain.
I go into an altered state of consciousness, poison!
Killing all in its path.
Hepatic Encephalopathy! Long stay then left,
warnings given, all in vain.
I met my "Friend" within the hour,
then others joined, an ugly aftermath!

Now to deal with my plumbing and legs. My nerves are burnt.
Walking is a chore, pain immense, no body control, what a mess!
The life that I have been given, I want another! There's a lot I learnt.
With home care, ambulance, and police, they all know my address.

Living on borrowed time, the battle raged on, totally powerless!
Pills galore, they were not needed, I knew better, I've my "Friends".
More organ failures, pancreas, bladder and bowels, not to impress.
Learn from me. Been hooked for forty-six years,
this is where it ends!

THE NURSES

Someone needed help, sick they were.
The hospital was the only choice.
She had been before and it wasn't for her.
She needed it, as she had no voice.

An emergency hospital visit was made.
The operations really opened my eyes.
There were many people on a crusade.
They worked tirelessly, without even sighs.

Through thick and thin they cared for the sick.
They are wonderful angels sent from the sky.
Yelling, crying, dying, they are tough as a brick.
How can they do it? Without a blink of an eye.

A simple smile can change anyone.
How they again rise above the rest.
Glad they're there, second to none.
I've watched enough to call them the best.

These men and women battle through diseases.
Risking their lives, their work is never done.
All day and night, the work never ceases,
Twelve hour shifts, the workload must weigh a ton

If you have not needed their service, I know I have.
Then please read again the verses.
We should be so eternally grateful and so glad.
To call the real heros, our NURSES!

PRETTY EYES

Sweep, sweep, wipe, take the garbage and mop.
One room done! Fifty more to go, so I watch.
From my hospital bed, my eyes open, she's nonstop.
Her day was done, homebound, time to wash.

They are the forgotten ones, the true heroes.
The yelling and rudeness on the floor, unknown?
She continued, one more just needs pillows.
Tired and needed some food and being alone.

While in my hospital bed, one entered, my eyes really open.
I've watched an angel enter my life
She had piercing eyes, I melted, was going to need oxygen.
Tongue tied, I thought of her as my wife.

I called her Pretty Eyes, but so much more.
She was cocky, outgoing, humorous, and had a body too!
Day after day, her job was cleaning her floor.
I hoped to always see her, if not I was gonna be blue!

LOVE LOST

Goodbye! Too little, too late!
The words I hated to hear.
But with me, it was simply fate.
I knew it was time to adhere.

The drink, my "Friend", had done a job.
It took shyness, but it only created a loss.
There I was, left alone living in a fog!
My "Friend", you were a controlling boss.

Sorry is such an overused word.
It meant nothing, only my actions work.
My "Friend" you made me absurd.
Wife and daughters gone, I went berserk!

I took a chance and lost my "Friend".
In good time my sober actions would show.
Fresh start. I could no longer pretend.
I'm an alcoholic!! I knew it would be slow.

Yesterday is dead, live today as tomorrow is yet alive.
I waited tearfully, but patiently, for my family to return.
With determination and work, I hoped they would arrive.
Love lost, emotional pain. Their return, I had to earn.

My wife long gave up hope in me since my "Friend" had returned!
I was shown the door. Well, the police assisted in this.
Was released from prison. Ordered to Ottawa.
I should have learned!
My family was gone!! I now entered a very dark abyss!

THE RIGHT SIDE
OF THE GRASS

One day I went upstairs.
While sitting in my usual chair.
The thoughts were monotone.
But deep enough to scare.

The day progressed well into the night.
The thoughts were so very deep.
I paced only thinking of immense fright.
My "Friend" would help me sleep.

I commenced hurting myself that day.
As I trusted my thoughts being alone
I really wanted to see myself decay.
Right down to my very last bone.

My "Friend", my lifelong, one true love.
You focused on my pain.
I knew it was the only one I had, my dove.
To fly me from insane.

Over and over I had tried.
But the lifelong pain still lingers.
Love lost, financial ruin, words lies.
All I had was my "Friend" in my fingers.

My entire body lies in ruin.
Are you that happy my "Friend".
How do I stop you menacing bruin?
From taking me to the end?

The sun rose years later behind a mask of cloud.
I realized that I could rise out of despair and find me.
I lost my deepest loving "Friend" and I am proud.
The feelings of visiting my maker vanished guarantee.

I know now there is a path and a way.
And the feelings slowly disappear.
My "Friend" I no longer obey.
Once controlled, I am now the puppeteer.

Walking the path well traveled, the leaves rustled underfoot.
With eyes open, seeking a great life for this old lass.
My dearest "Friend" forty-six years later, you I finally unhook.
I want to live on the **Right Side Of The Grass.**

THE DREADED THOUGHTS

How I hate this moment bringing this to the surface.
I am a dead soul rebuilding my existence and purpose.
There were many a day dying within my fortress.
My spinning thoughts and fear, creating my hell circus.

Your upstairs is a very dangerous place to venture.
I've gone and continue to unfortunately go.
Time for healing! I left it for last, This chapter has no splendor!
Hopeful of death, those times were never a glow!

Tried and tried to go silently, I feared no death.
I wanted for my hell to end now.
I awoke, fuck! I was still here. I was a little distressed.
But I wanted to go, so why not allow.

Fearful of my capabilities and my warped reality.
I hid, cried, and I was dying inside, I had no way out.
Always, always heard "you're great socially"!
Far from reality but others said I had nothing to fear about.

My wall was enormous, never letting fear be shown.
Inner peace and tranquility, I was always looking for.
I chose the easy option, more than anyone had ever known.
Took all my "Friends" at once in quantities galore.

Strapped to the bed, police at my side, what happened?
I failed! My hell was supposed to end, now just utter despair,
"You are not going home" was heard, freedom felt threatened.
Seventy two hour minimum hold by law, felt beyond repair.

Not really sober but I went home, I wanted to get to the end.
Again everything devoured, to stay sober nah! Never works.
More psychiatrist visits, more meds, It was hard to comprehend.
This poem was hardest to write, to the core with lots of waterworks.

Nothing ever stopped my desire, Suicide tried again.
My thoughts stuck within my skin.
I had new tactics, death by cop, to finally end my pain.
Those that saw me did not know my twin.

I never was able to do it, so someone will.
I threaten cops and get tackled, then my hell escalates.
I'm back to the psychiatry ward. and many a pill.
Released to battle again, was only trying to reach heaven's gates.

In my reality, there was only a chance at peace.
It was to finally meet my maker at any cost.
For I remember that feeling never cease.
My "Friends" continuing my life long holocaust.

My "Upstairs! Hamster, GET OFF the fucking wheel.
Spinning out of control and wanting to die.
Every effort made to ruin everything, I was given a deal.
Dad, "we will help, we cannot continue to cry".

I'm sober now, but "Upstairs" is still a daily threat.
Managed properly with self love, patience and peace.
Clear mind, growth, calm, with time acquired as a set.
I'm wise enough to know this will continue until I decease.

REHAB

No, No, I promise I didn't use.
Obviously, others saw the truth.
Me? Nothing seen, in full abuse.
Drinking daily, my Rye and Vermouth.

Rehab, why? I was alright, I believed I was fine.
My activation of denial, internal demons.
Anger, crying, despair my "Friend" and I confine.
No problem, I again performed deceptions.

Kicking, screaming as I was to meet "The Door".
A shell, a wall, an onion to be peeled.
Hiding, crying, thinking I'm alone, I needed to restore.
My social breakdown. I kept concealed.

Groups and classes, activities and more.
My feelings altered, friends made, my ears wide open.
I was releasing emotions deep in my core.
My true soul emerges. Hey, I was becoming unbroken.

Walking the same path from different pasts.
Sharing inner secrets to strangers I don't even know.
They become family, together adrift on our rafts.
Family, counselors, and all who share. You I owe.

From broken souls at the door of life, pain,
suffering, angry, and scared.
My core was full! I unhooked only one at a time.
All my loves lost, demons, regrets and more all emotionally shared.
Knowledge taken, now it's a slow and steady climb.

There is work to do, and the real journey begins.
The foundation was built, now I was left on my own.
Reactivation of life, I now have many a grin.
A life of sobriety and self discovery, rehab has shown.

POSITIVITY

Everyday life throws you many curveballs.
They are not to be ignored but rather embraced.
Take time to process just watching the walls.
Every obstacle is a growth and problem erased.

The sun will always rise, so please take delight.
Your "Upstairs" properly managed if it was filled.
On the right side of the grass, living in calm white.
No complaining, change your thinking, be thrilled.

A choice: To think and be positive or hurt and suffer.
It's quite easy, just let go, find clarity, and upgrade your mind.
Be present, aware of your thoughts and discover.
Find pleasure, smile and laugh! Leave the negative behind.

Awake, make the bed, shower, and dress, find satisfaction.
Now look and talk in the mirror and what do you see? and hear?
A beautiful person, but what you say and hear takes traction.
Continue this every day and soon happiness comes, do not veer!

It is said "a thousand actions make a reaction"
Any negativity, mirror reinforced repeatedly, you're done!
Why? Pain and suffering, what's the attraction?
Take a step forward and never back, living in yesterday is never fun.

I learned so much from the hurt and pain.
Let me utilize my knowledge and free myself from dissension.
Being alone, I don't venture "Upstairs", as it is in vain.
I know and believe, it is time for me to find my life reinvention.

WHAT'S DONE, IS DONE

We spend most of our daily time thinking.
Most days are taken over in yesterday.
Why use thoughts that allow us to be sinking?
Our thoughts should never be gray.

Yesterday is always dead, what's done, is done.
We always ruminate in What if? What if?
Do those thoughts compile positively? Not one!
The pain, tears, anger and we go adrift!

Commence your day with happiness and smiles, not tears.
Every day is easy if you completely ease your mind.
It's no longer your business what transpired over the years.
For it is yesterday, your thoughts, you shouldn't find.

Remember that tomorrow is yet alive.
The past is definitely the past.
There's a place your thoughts can thrive.
The present! Do this as life is fast!

THE COSTS

The costs were staggering, I know we all think one thing.
Reality hit, my buddies, my wife and children were gone!
Those were huge costs, now sober, I hope for an upswing!
Financially, wow! Debt, I was now collecting things to pawn.

With no family but cash from the sale of the house, I spent.
Buying love, my "Friends", and toys, all for self gratification.
I wasn't talking to kids. University will cost when they attend.
I ceased being selfish, saved for their educational foundation.

It is now time to discuss my finances. Fuck I don't know how!
I figured thirty-five to sixty grand a year.
I didn't want to do the math!
It was fucking nuts! Yesterday was dead, nothing stopping me now.
My wealth was not measured by cash but by my insane life path.

I definitely took a wrong turn. This path really sucks!
I had two homes, one was free but came with a cost.
Organ failures, constant poisoning, pills for a few bucks.
The stigma, my reputation, I'm in my very own holocaust.

The steps needed to be taken, it was time for amends.
The costs were very high, the timing was of the extreme essence.
They may not be ready, me either! Especially my friends.
Family may understand, since I have had this since my adolescence.

I accepted the costs, no one could have lived with me.
I was always with my "Friend" as years passed on.
For today is what is important, where I can be free
It's really nice!, Considering I should be gone.

RECOVERY

Detox at rehab, Hell, I couldn't retreat, step one admitted!
I burned a few demons and the foundation was again laid.
Forty five days, I learned but no success if not committed.
That day came and I left yesterday behind, not being afraid!

Left feeling confident,
but I knew my "Friend" was always searching.
My lost bottles were found! I was scared! I needed an escape plan!
Living alone, sheer boredom, Covid,
a call list made in case of urging.
Writing now, demons occupy "Upstairs",
slowly burning, will be a span.

Gone are those days of taking the cap off never to be seen again.
Fucking insanity, forty-six years of waking
to a mask of clouds, in despair!
I was seeking splendor, it's possible, HELL YA ! It's worth the pain.
Every day a blessing. I continued to do mirror talks,
and now do a dare.

Addiction is a nasty persistent demon weaving through generations.
It wounds, scars, scares, everyone it meets, but that is yesterday!
With tomorrow yet alive, we're left with
what's built on our foundations.
Keep busy, stay focused, be bold, be wise,
set boundaries and don't sway.

Live by the 7 **P**'s, **P**rior **P**roper **P**lanning **P**revents
Piss **P**oor **P**erformance
Words to remember, words to practice,
words to ward off disappointment.
With a proper plan, tackle resentment and anger,
with full conformance!
Slowly peace and contentment will follow,
yesterday only by appointment.

Start a routine, first make your bed, feelings of accomplishment!
Stay connected, practice what you were taught,
fight the fight from hell.
Remember to live for today, stay positive, thoughts of astonishment.
Now a few months of sober living, no other way to live,
I shall be well.

Time to take action! Reverse some damage that was self-inflicted.
New diet, walks, writing, the right plan,
and routine all doing their part.
No one said it would be easy! What's done, is done!
I was not conflicted.
My journey is very active, I needed this, to repair my crushed heart!

MY GIRLS

May, 2002. The day I was blessed with true love.
The first time I saw her, tears of joy flowed.
She was so small that I held her like a glove.
All smiles and fear, we took her back to our abode.

Dad was so proud and dressed her up.
I always took her shopping for all to see.
I learned very quickly, this is not like raising a pup.
She was named Peyton, we wanted three.

In July 2004, there were two, when my princess Paige was born
The instant I saw her face, I remember seeing me.
She was beautiful, with those cute little dimples she adorned.
I had my two little Girls, one in my arm and the other on my knee.

I was a great dad , always loving, affectionate, and playful.
I couldn't get enough of them,
their unconditional love consumed me.
My "Friend" would show up, but I really tried to remain faithful.
My girls always would come first, as I let out my first "Friend" plea.

The plea did not work, my "Friend" hooked me again stronger.
Soon I had forgotten the two most important people in my life
My "Friend", the bottle, had won,
I couldn't live with both any longer.
As my insane, unimaginable battle raged on,
my kids left with my wife.

Left alone for my "Friends" to visit, I forgot about my girls.
Through anger, crying, throwing, and hospital detoxes they tried.
I abandoned them and chose my "Friend" over my pearls.
The thoughts of my hurtful actions! I wish I would have died.

I remember when I was court ordered to live away.
Watching them cry and roll in the ditch. It elevated my hurt.
I caused that hurt and many more, alone I now pray.
They will never forget the hell; They were old enough to be alert.

I loved my girls with every part of my being, always on my mind.
Their smiles melt hearts, capturing audiences
with sparkle in their eyes.
This poem is for you two, the best daughters, one of a kind.
I am truly sorry girls for it was not me, but something
I now despise.

DESPAIR

Walked and walked, his destination was unknown.
Night near, shelter sought, he was feeling helpless.
Eyes searching, concrete corner, in comfort, NO!
What has happened to him? He was the eldest.

The Morning arose, the heat was felt, his next walk.
Shopping cart filled, he was hungry and was going to yack.
Wandering, tremors, liquor store closed, started to gawk!!
He needed his daily "Friend" and It wanted him back.

At Storefront, cardboard sign, hands in the air.
Seeking just enough money to grab his "Friend".
Gulp, Gulp, AHH! The shakes were gone, now where?
The cycle continued, it may take him to the end.

Tonight's home was found, his house in cart assembled.
His fingers tightly wrapped around his "Friend".
Dreaded "Upstairs" created thoughts, while he trembled.
Thought he was a loser, worthless. Will it take him to the end!

He was a lost sole, stricken with guilt and shame.
Shredded clothes, ratty old blanket, and he smelled like shit.
Huddled up in a ball, lying in public, this was no game!
His survival for a homeless alcoholic, like me, I wished he
would quit.

Took him to the hospital and an admission was made.
His serious despair, the despair, the despair!
Step one commenced, his "Friend" got the blade.
The ending? His journey had begun so I am not aware

FINAL WORDS

I hope you were able to feel the power of addiction and its causes and costs. I drank for 46 years of my life and have not had it easy.

I was born into a great family and was fully loved and supported. I found myself drawn to the people having fun at social get-togethers. What was their secret to happiness? They always had drinks and smokes. I found myself trying both one night and getting instantly into another dimension. I could talk, laugh and have fun.

Well what a let down that is now forty-six years later! A nightmare of a journey in addiction. My addiction led me to dark places and changed the path of life I had envisioned. It just seems if I had it too good, I would find a way to ruin it. I seemed to enjoy misery.

Hospital stays became frequent. I was called the walking dead as I had alcohol levels twice the danger zone and that would kill others and still I was walking (probably not well). On top of the continued abuse, my kidneys died, my liver failed and many other life threatening ailments and conditions have come on due to the alcohol abuse.

It took me 4 rehab centre visits to finally let my "Friend" alcohol go. I remain positive everyday even with my ailments that afflict me. Walking is a chore and pain is intense. Drivers licence suspended due to medical conditions, so loss of freedom.

This is one chapter that never ends as the struggle continues every day!

I am a few months into my recovery and I have never been so clear headed and for the first time in my life, I am starting to really be free and happy.

I have found my outlet for emotions and demons coming to surface. I write about it in a poem. These poems are my life and I don't want anyone to follow it but I am a realist as a new person is hooked every minute. If my words help one person then I have already done my job as it has helped me and at this point of my journey my recovery comes first.

Thank you and God Bless

CPSIA information can be obtained
at www.ICGtesting.com
Printed in the USA
LVHW101117030822
724959LV00006B/252